The Evergreen Art of Banana Leaf Folding

Eclectic Celebration in Green

Rajani Ramkumar ★ Malathi Satish ★ Chatura Ajith ★ Uma Balaji

ISBN
Paperback 979-8-89673-459-8
Hardcase 979-8-89699-323-0

- Cultural Symbolism
- Creative Expression
- Handcrafted Beauty
- Versatile Medium
- Traditional Design
- Eco-Friendly Material

Green Gold

A craft that bridges Tradition and Contemporary styles.

"Loy Krathong" in Thailand is a time-honoured, traditional art form of banana leaf folding, deeply rooted in its Thai / Buddhist culture and history. The technique of banana leaf folding is steeped in spirituality. This is an ancient practice which involves intricately and painstakingly folding banana leaves for religious rituals, festive occasions and social events.

In our Indian way of life, banana leaves symbolizes auspiciousness and are believed to bring good fortune and prosperity. The art of working with banana leaves creates intricate patterns and holds profound cultural importance for Indians.

Banana leaf folding embodies the quintessence of environmental stewardship and sustenance, far beyond its cultural and functional significance. Through its elaborate detailed designs, ethnic importance and habitual, practical and eco-friendly applications, it serves as a tangible expression of our rich heritage and lasting traditions.

Foreword

Welcome to the world of art in another hue and form. The world has an array of cultures and our country is both ancient and unique. The uses of plants like banana, coconut, mango, neem and more, as part of food, health or décor has been around for centuries. The banana plant is one such, which lends itself to décor, be it the pith or leaves.

'The Evergreen Art of Banana Leaf Folding' shows a myriad ways of maneuvering the leaf to create designs for not only traditional, cultural occasions but also contemporary and functional ones. Simple ones for beginners in the art to be motivated to learn and advanced ways to inspire are included in the following pages. Garlands, trays, frames, shapes of flowers, birds that are suitable for the table top, wall, doorways and enhancing traditional figurines can be seen.

The versatile material and ideas of the creators can move your hands into becoming deft and nimble. It will help improve the concentration skill and attention span of both adults and children. Much needed in today's fast-paced world.

My congratulations and good wishes to the innovative team of Art Crumps-Chatura Ajith, Rajani Ramkumar, Uma Balaji and Malathi Satish on the new book. This kind of sustainable art is evergreen indeed!

Ohryu Rekha Reddy
Sub Grandmaster
Ohara Ikebana, Hyderabad

Annexure ABC

A. Supportive pointers

1. Select tender, bright green banana leaves.

2. Cut the centre stem and wipe the leaves clean.

3. Cut the leaves into the required size, mostly 1.5" to 2" width. The lesser the width, the more intricate the design.

4. Ensure all foldings are of uniform size and preferably the same colour.

5. Foldings can be prepared in advance and stored in a polythene cover in the fridge for a day or two.

6. Staples should not be visible when your design is complete. It can be concealed by using Zig Zag fold or a ribbon.

7. Keep spraying water at least three times a day for longer life.

8. The shape, size, and thickness of the thermocol/styrofoam/banana stem used for each design can be varied.

9. Conceal the base completely with banana leaf/tissue cloth, and the edges with tissue/satin ribbons.

B. Required supplies

Banana leaves

Thermocol/Styrofoam/Banana stem

Knife to cut the base

Scissors

Stapler & staple pins

Ribbons – Satin/Tissue

Bell/head pins

Tooth picks

Adhesive

C. Add – Ons

Beads/pearls

Gigantea Buds (Crown Flower)

Montana buds (Erva Tamia Tabernaemontana buds)

Yellow tender leaves from the coconut palm

Rose/orchid petals

Flowers

Decorative pins

1. Trifold

Pg. No. 7

2. Trinity

Pg. No. 8

3. Envelope

Pg. No. 9

4. Twirl

Pg. No. 10

5. Array

Pg. No. 11

6. Arrow Head

Pg. No. 12

7. Arrow Twist

Pg. No. 13

8. Rocket

Pg. No. 14

9. Pointers

Pg. No. 15

10. Zig Zag

Pg. No. 16

11. Zee

Pg. No. 17 & 18

12. Cone

Pg. No. 19

13. Coronet

Pg. No. 20

14. Temple

Pg. No. 21

15. Embellish

Pg. No. 22

16. Collar

Pg. No. 23

17. Collar Remix

Pg. No. 24

18. Dragon Tail

Pg. No. 25

19. Dragon Twist

Pg. No. 26

20. Lavish

Pg. No. 27

21. Twin Cone

Pg. No. 28

22. Ruffles

Pg. No. 29

23. Cascade

Pg. No. 30

24. Bud

Pg. No. 31

25. 3D Mini

Pg. No. 32

1 : Trifold

Hold the strip horizontally with both hands.

Fold upto 3/4 of the length of the leaf from the left.

Fold the remaining 1/4 portion parallel to the first fold, as shown.

Ensure the folded ends are next to each other.

Fold the right portion further towards the centre.

Ensure the fold line of the leaf is perfectly centred.

Staple at the centre of the bottom edge to secure the folds in place.

Trim the bottom edge of the leaf into a straight line.

2 : Trinity

Hold the strip horizontally using both hands.

Fold it downwards from the right at a 90-degree angle.

Repeat the fold on left side to form an equilateral triangle.

Cut off the extra leaf and staple in the centre, as low as possible, to hold the folds together.

This folding can be used individually or in layers, placing each slightly lower than the previous one.

3. Envelope

Hold the strip horizontally with both hands.

Fold it downwards from the centre at a 90-degree angle.

Repeat on the other side to form a triangle.

Fold the right edge of the triangle slightly away from the centre.

Repeat on the left edge.

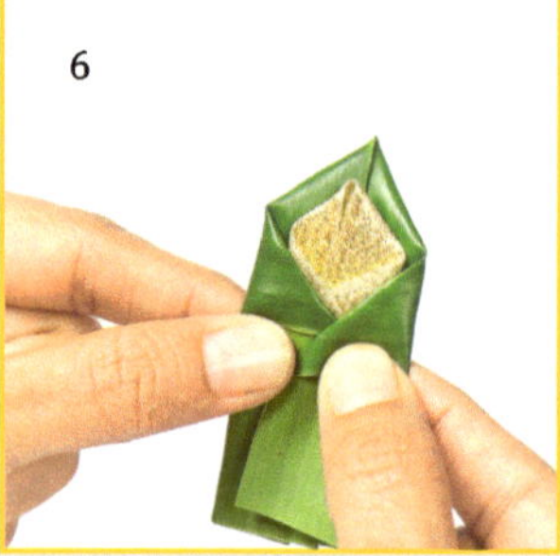

Option 1: Place a piece of 1/2-inch ribbon folded like an envelope.

Option 2: Before making the second fold, insert an inverted, folded rose petal.

Note: This folding technique can also be created using Arrow Head folding.

4. Twirl

1

Hold the strip horizontally with both hands.

2

Fold the right side downward at a 90-degree angle.

3

Repeat the same fold on the left side.

4

Fold the strip backward and bring both ends together.

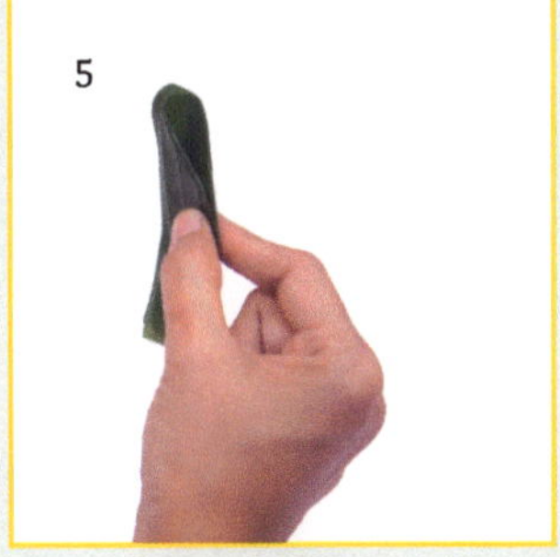

5

Create another fold in the same way, ensuring both ends are aligned.

6

Insert this folded piece into the first one and secure it with a staple pin.

7

Continue this pattern until the desired length is achieved.

5. Array

Hold the strip horizontally with both hands.

Fold it down from the right at a 90-degree angle.

Repeat on the opposite side to form an equilateral triangle.

Fold it in the centre to form a right-angled triangle.

Make another similar folding and insert it into the first folding. Staple at the bottom to hold them together.

Continue these steps until the desired length is reached. Cut the extra leaf, leaving half an inch at the base.

6. Arrow Head

Hold the strip horizontally with both hands.

Fold the strip from both edges, creating two tapers that meet at the centre.

Fold the right portion further towards the centre to form a 90-degree angle.

Repeat on the other side to form a triangle. Cut off the extra leaf and staple it at the bottom to secure the folds.

This folding can be used individually or in layers, placing each fold 1/4 inch lower than the previous one.

Note: If using in layers, use a strip 1/4 inch narrower in width for each subsequent folding.

7. Arrow Twist

Hold the strip horizontally with both hands.

Fold each end of the strip at a 45-degree angle.

Fold it again at a 90-degree angle to form a triangle shape.

Fold both ends backward so they meet at the centre. The left-side image shows the back view, while the right-side image shows the front view. Staple it at the bottom.

8. Rocket

Hold the strip horizontally with both hands.

Fold each end at a 45-degree angle.

Fold each end again at a 90-degree angle to form a triangle.

Flip the folding over and fold both ends so they overlap. Secure the overlap with a staple pin.

9. Pointers

Hold the strip horizontally with both hands.

Fold the right end inward from the centre of the strip at an angle slightly greater than 90 degrees.

Fold the left side to align with the previous fold.

Trim any excess leaf and staple it at the centre.

Create similar foldings and layer them one over the other, leaving a 1/4" gap between each layer. Repeat until the desired length is achieved, then trim the sides for a neat finish.

This folding technique is often used alongside larger foldings.

10. Zig Zag

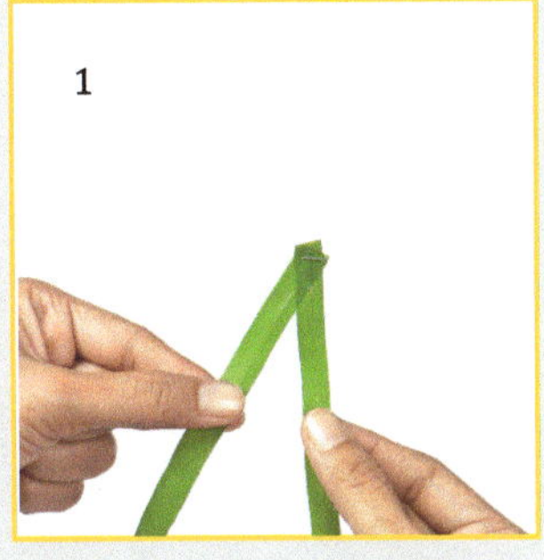

Take two strips of banana leaf, each 1/2" wide. Hold them in an inverted V shape and secure them with a staple.

Bring the left strip over the right strip to form a peak at the centre.

Continue interlacing the strips in the same manner until the end, then staple to secure.

This zig-zag folding is typically used to cover the unfinished edges of a design.

Note: This folding can also be done using satin or tissue ribbons. It can be created directly on your finished design by following the same steps. For better stability, it is recommended to use a bell pin / pearl-headed pin after forming each peak.

11. Zee

Fold both sides of the banana leaf strip from the centre at a 90-degree angle to form a triangle.

Fold it again at the centre to create a right-angled triangle.

Hold the strip horizontally with the pointed edge facing the left.

Fold the top loose end of the strip downward to align with the base of the triangle.

Repeat the same step on the other side.

11. Zee

Fold the right side of the strip over the triangle toward the left. Repeat this process on the opposite side to complete the Zee folding.

Open the folding.

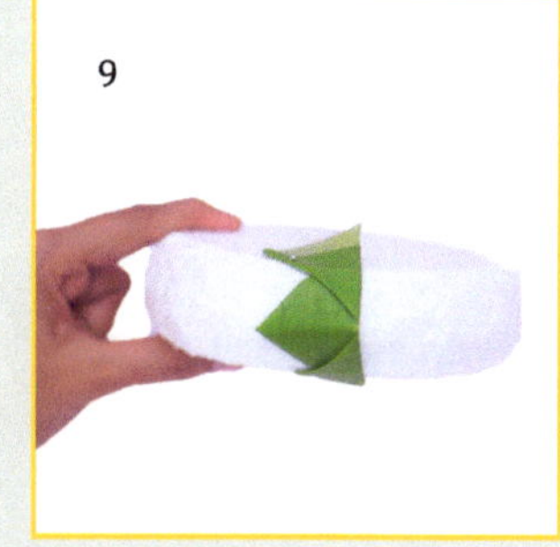

Attach the folding to the round-edged base and secure it at both ends.

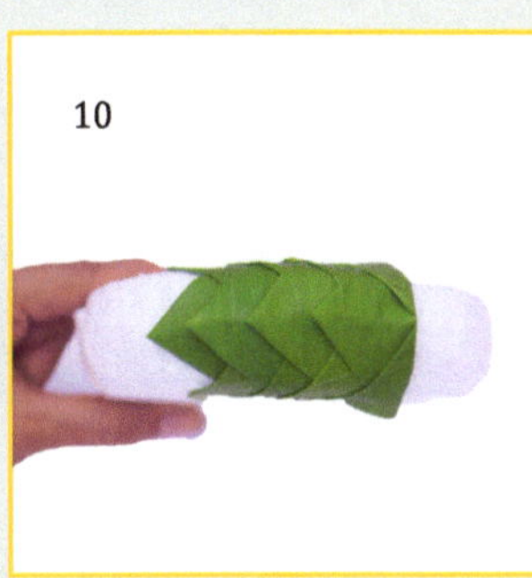

Using the same method, continue attaching foldings at 1/2" intervals until the circle is completely covered.

Variation: Fold the top layer to the right, insert the second folding into the first, and staple it at the bottom. Repeat this sequence until the desired length is achieved. This can be used to fix it to the sides of the base.

12. Cone

Hold the strip horizontally with both hands, ensuring the softer side of the leaf is on the right.

Tightly roll the top right corner toward the centre.

Continue rolling the strip firmly.

Roll until the left edge is reached.

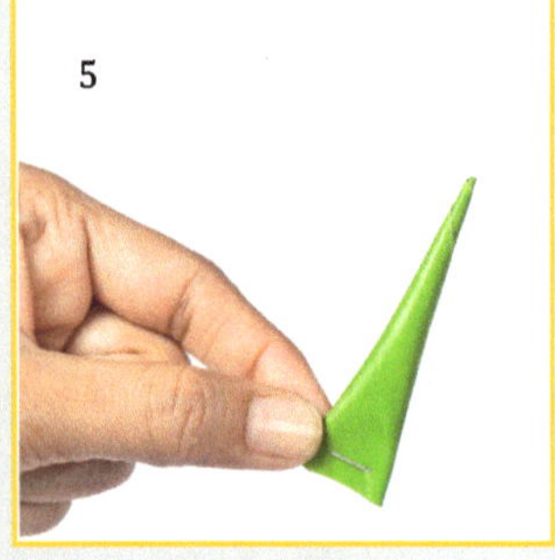

Secure the cone with a staple and trim any excess leaf at the bottom.

This folding can be used individually or stacked with 1/4" gaps between each cone, pinned securely.

13. Coronet

Insert a cone between the two layers of the Array folding.

Insert another Array folding from the right side, ensuring it overlaps the first one.

Secure the fold with a staple and trim the excess leaf at the bottom.

Create a second layer by inserting two additional Array foldings on either side.

Staple the layers and trim any excess leaf.

14. Temple

Insert a cone between the two layers of an Array folding, positioning it close to the cone.

Add another Array folding from the right side, placing it close to the cone and overlapping the previous one. Secure it with a staple.

Repeat this process, leaving a quarter inch gap each time, until you reach the desired length. Trim any excess leaf at the bottom.

15. Embellish

This folding is similar to the Temple folding, but cones are added at every step.

After completing the folding, you can enhance it by adding pearl-headed pins to the pointed ends of the cones.

If using Montana buds, insert them into the first fold of the cones and roll them securely.

16. Collar

Hold the strip horizontally with both hands.

Place a cone at the centre of the strip and fold both sides of the leaf at a 45-degree angle.

Wrap the right side of the leaf around the cone.

Wrap the left side of the leaf, overlapping the previous fold, and secure it at the bottom with a staple.

Repeat the process, leaving a quarter inch gap each time, until u reach the desired length.

17. Collar Remix

Place a cone at the centre of a strip of banana leaf.

Fold the right side of the strip alongside the cone.

Bring the fold closer to the cone and fold it outward.

Repeat the process on the left side.

Continue alternating the folds, placing each half inch lower on each side, until the desired length is achieved.

18. Dragon Tail

Hold a strip of banana leaf horizontally.

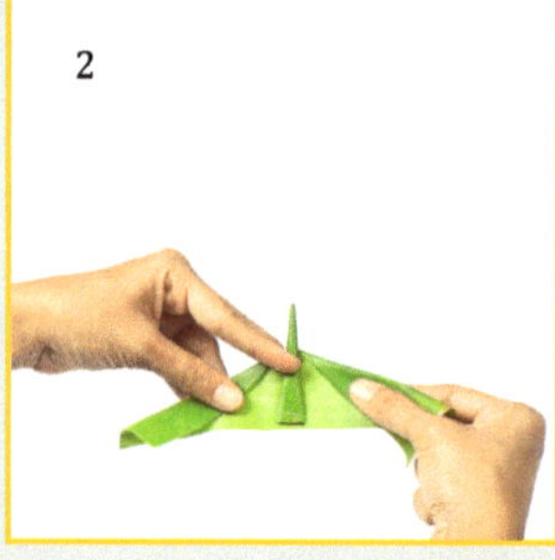

Place a cone at the centre of the strip and fold both sides at a 45-degree angle.

Wrap the right side of the leaf around the cone.

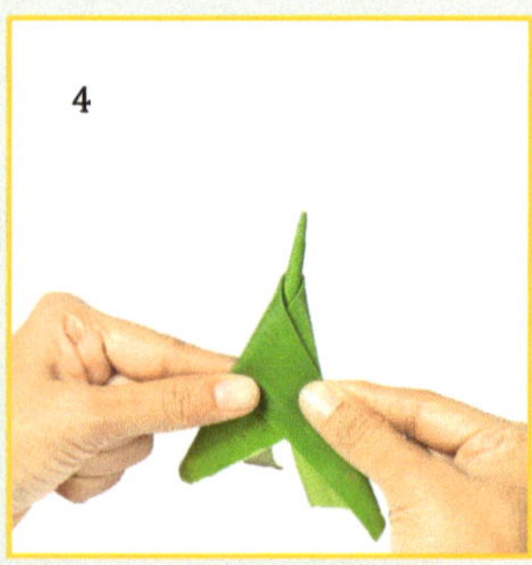

Wrap the left side of the leaf around the cone and secure it with a staple.

Place another cone 1/2" below the previous one and repeat the wrapping process.

Continue this pattern until the desired length is achieved.

19. Dragon Twist

Place a cone at the centre of a strip.

Fold the right side of the strip alongside the cone.

Wrap it close to the cone and fold it outward.

Repeat the process on the left side.

Position the next cone half inch below the previous one and wrap it in the same manner. Continue this process until the desired length is achieved.

20. Lavish

Prepare two cones using Montana buds and staple them together, leaving a 1/2" gap between them.

Place the cones on a 1 1/2"-wide strip of banana leaf, positioning the longer cone toward you. Fold the right side of the leaf at a 45-degree angle.

Wrap the leaf close to the cone.

Repeat the process on the left side, tucking any extra leaf inward for a clean finish.

Flip it over and position a third cone 1/2" below the shorter cone. Turn it again and wrap it with the banana leaf. Flip it back, add a fourth cone below the third, and wrap it again.

Continue flipping, adding cones, and wrapping with the banana leaf until you reach your desired length.

21. Twin Cone

Hold the strip horizontally with both hands.

Roll each end of the strip tightly toward the centre.

Continue rolling until both ends meet at the centre.

Secure with a staple and trim any excess leaf from the bottom.

22. Ruffles

Hold the strip horizontally with both hands.

Fold it in half horizontally.

Start by making a pleat leaving about 1" from the left end.

Create a second pleat next to the first one.

Continue pleating along the length of the leaf.

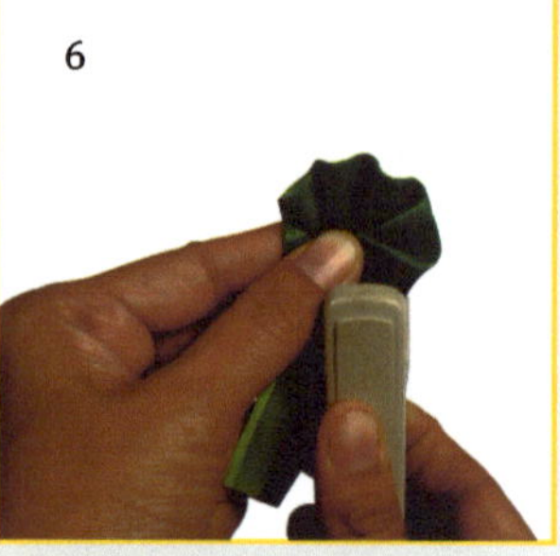

Secure the pleats with at least two staples.

Trim any excess leaf neatly.

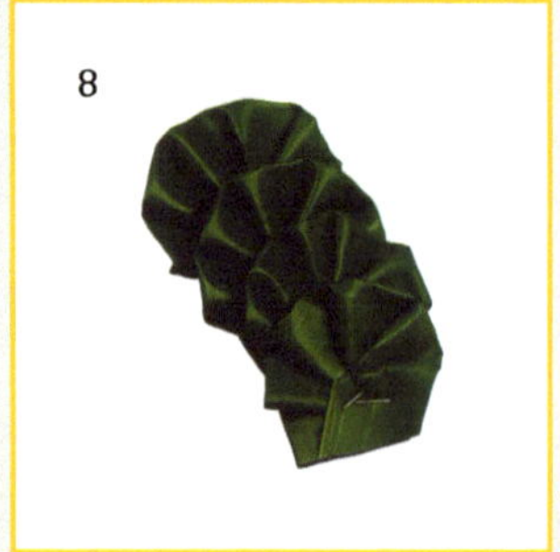

Repeat the process to make as many pieces as needed. While fixing them ensure the staples are concealed.

23. Cascade

Start with a 2" strip of banana leaf, holding it horizontally with both hands.

Fold the strip in half horizontally. Create a pleat on the left side with the top layer of the leaf.

Make a similar pleat on the right side.

Overlap both ends and secure them with a staple. This creates a single-step version of the cascade fold.

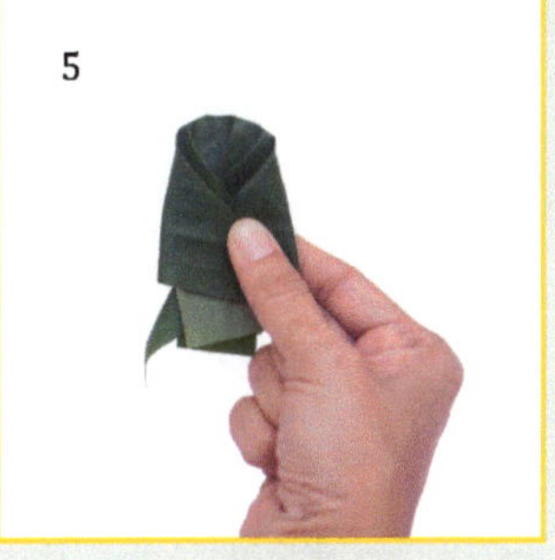

For another variation, add an additional layer of pleats before overlapping and securing the ends.

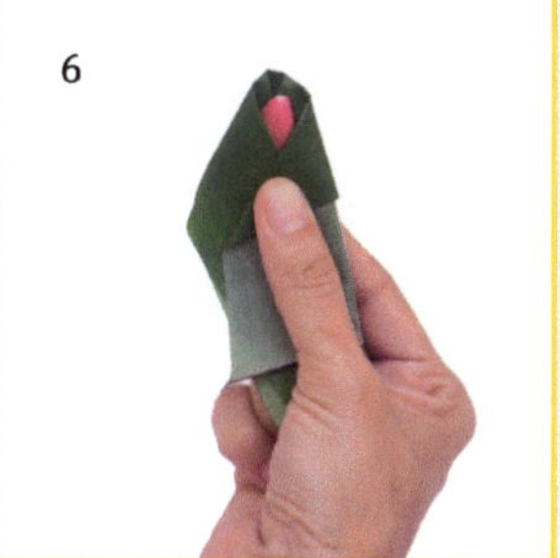

Optionally, insert a rose petal after pleating for added detail.

24. Bud

Start with a strip of banana leaf measuring 2.5" to 3" in width.

Fold the leaf in half horizontally.

Hold the folded strip in your left hand, and with your right forefinger, push the seam of the fold toward the centre.

While keeping the right fold in place, repeat the process on the left side to form a neat triangle.

Fold the top layer from the right side toward the left.

Similarly, fold the top layer from the left side toward the right.

Wrap the remaining double fold of the leaf to form a second layer.

Secure the folds with a staple and trim to the desired length.

25. 3D Mini

Take a 1" wide banana leaf strip and hold it horizontally with both hands.

Fold the strip in half horizontally.

Twist the left side of the leaf at a 45-degree angle downward.

Twist the right side of the leaf parallel to the left, moving from bottom to top.

Twist the right side again, this time from top to bottom backward, keeping it parallel to the left twist.

Fold the first twist on the left downward so it faces down.

Fold the middle of the right twist backward, aligning it parallel to the left fold.

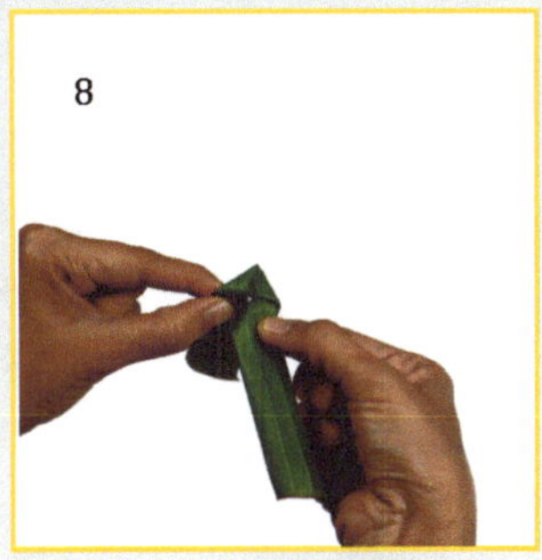

Lift the right fold and place it over the left fold to form a peak.

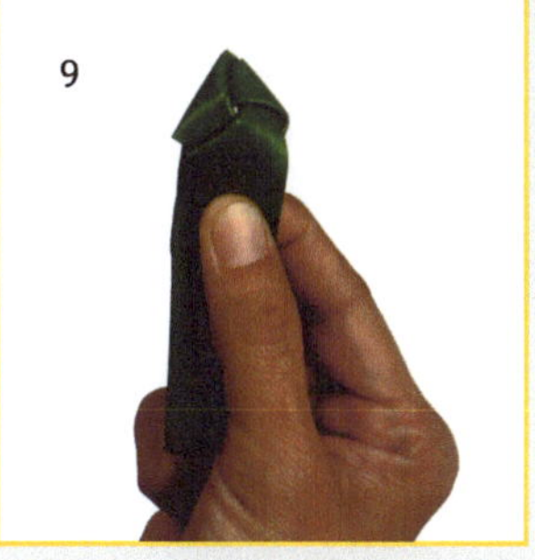

Secure with a staple and trim the excess just below the staple.

Star Blossom

Step 1: Preparing the Base

A) Start with an 8-inch diameter, 1-inch thick thermocol circle. Cover the base of the thermocol with two layers of banana leaf. Wrap a satin or tissue ribbon around the side for a neat finish.

Step 2: Preparing the Foldings

A) Use both dark and light-coloured banana leaves for visual contrast.

B) For the first row, cut 3-inch wide strips of banana leaf. Reduce the width by 1/2 inch for each of the next two consecutive rows.

C) Prepare approximately 14 sets of three Arrowhead foldings, layering them 1/4th inch below each other, with the light-coloured folding in the centre.

D) Trim the extra portion at the bottom of the largest set of foldings. Use one folding as a template to cut the remaining foldings to ensure uniformity.

Step 3: Fixing the Foldings

A) Begin by fixing the foldings 1/2 inch from the edge of the thermocol using head pins on both sides of the foldings. Arrange them next to each other to complete the circle.

B) For the next row, use the set of foldings that are 1/2 inch smaller than the first set. Trim them uniformly at the bottom. Fix these foldings in between the foldings of the first row, placing them 1/2 inch away from the first row.

C) Repeat the process for the third and fourth rows using 2-inch and 1 1/2-inch sets of foldings, respectively.

D) For the final touch, fix folded rose petals over the pins from the previous row to conceal them. In the centre, arrange a cluster of gigantea flowers to cover all the pins from the rose petals row, completing the design.

6. Arrow Head

Leaf Majesty

Two-Tier Design Instructions

Materials:
- 1-inch thick thermocol piece of 10-inch diameter (Base 1)
- 1 1/2-inch thick thermocol piece of 6-inch diameter (Base 2)
- Tissue fabric
- Gold-colored tissue ribbon
- Decorative golden beads
- Head pins
- Cylindrical container or banana stem (6 inches height)

Preparation:
1. Cover both thermocol circles with tissue fabric.
2. Fix a Zigzag folding with gold-coloured tissue ribbon along the top outer edge of each circle, pinning decorative golden beads between the peaks of the foldings.
3. Wrap and fix a gold tissue ribbon around the sides of both thermocol bases.

Base 1:
A) Prepare approximately 15 sets of Embellish foldings. Each set should have five cones decorated with golden beads.

B) Prepare 15 pieces of Envelope foldings, each with a rose petal inserted inside.

C) Trim the extra portion at the bottom of one Embellish folding and use it as a template to cut the remaining foldings for uniformity.

D) Fix the Embellish foldings upright along the outer edge of the circle using head pins on both ends. Continue placing them next to each other until the circle is complete.

E) Fix the envelope foldings in between the Embellish foldings.

F) Wrap a gold tissue ribbon around the bottom edge of Base 1 to cover the pins.

Base 2:
A) Prepare three rows of Envelope foldings. Each row should have 20-25 pieces, with rose petals inserted in the second row of foldings.

B) Begin by fixing plain Envelope foldings along the top edge of the circle, leaving a 1/2-inch gap from the top, placing them next to each other.

C) For the second row, position the Envelopes with rose petals in between the Envelopes of the first row.

D) For the third row, fix plain Envelopes in between the foldings of the second row.

E) Finish the outer edge of the third row by wrapping a gold tissue ribbon to cover the pins of the third row.

F) Position a cylindrical container or banana stem of 6-inch height in the centre of Base 1 to hold Base 2.

Circles of Elegance

Step 1:

Take a thermocol circle that is 1½ inches thick and 10" in diameter. Smoothen the edges to achieve a rounded finish. Use a Zee folding technique to cover the sides of the thermocol. Begin fixing the Zee foldings along the sides, securing both ends with bell pins. Continue attaching the Zee foldings until the entire perimeter is covered.

Step 2:

Prepare 25-30 Ruffles foldings for the next step. Attach the Ruffles slightly overlapping the Zee foldings to ensure the pins are concealed. Pin the Ruffles in a circular pattern, making sure to overlap each folding slightly to conceal the pins of the previous folding.

Step 3:

For the third layer, prepare 10 -12 Envelope foldings. Insert an orchid petal into each folding as you create them. Fix these Envelope foldings close to the Ruffles layer, ensuring a cohesive and decorative arrangement.

Step 4:

Take a small round thermocol piece, approximately 2 inches in diameter. Cover its top with two layers of banana leaf. Create a chain using the Array folding technique and attach it around the sides of the circle. Conceal the pins with a gold tissue ribbon for a polished look. Finally, place this circular piece in the centre of the design.

Note:

This arrangement is ideal for use as a ring platter or as a decorative piece.

Stellar Beauty

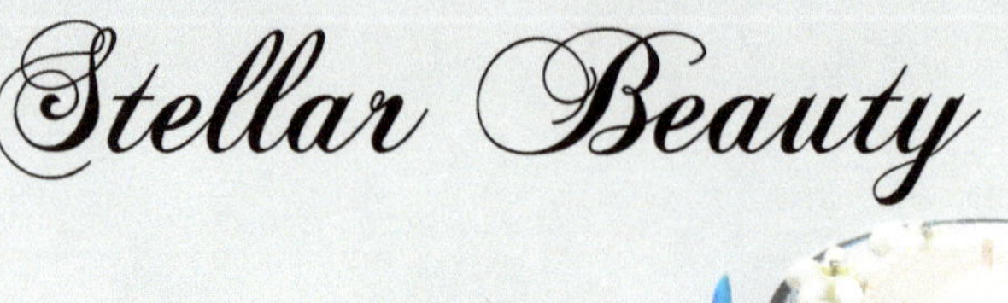

Bird's eye view

Step 1:
Take a thermocol circle with a thickness of 1½ inches and a diameter of 10 inches. Smoothen the edges to create a rounded finish. Use a Zee folding technique to cover the sides of the thermocol, ensuring the entire perimeter is covered neatly.

Step 2:
Prepare two sizes of cones using banana leaf strips—2½ inches and 2 inches in width. Insert Montana buds into the cones as you make them.

Step 3:
Use a cylindrical base with a diameter of 4-5 inches as a support. Flip the thermocol circle and rest it on this base. Begin attaching the smaller Cones with slight gaps between them. Once completed, fix the larger Cones in between the smaller ones. Flip the design back to its original position.

Step 4:
Conceal the edges of the Zee folding by fixing Zig Zag folding using an 1/2" ribbon.

Step 5:
To create Trifold sets: Cut banana leaf strips in five sizes, starting with 2½ inches width and reducing by ¼ inch for each of the next four sizes.

To assemble one set, begin with the largest Trifold and staple the subsequent ones on top, leaving a small gap near the pointed ends.

Prepare 9-10 such sets. Trim the extra leaf at the bottom of one set, and use it as a template to trim the rest to uniform size.

Step 6:
Fix the Trifold sets in a circular pattern, overlapping them slightly to form a complete circle.

Step 7:
Place a candle stand or a decorative piece in the centre of the design to complete the arrangement.

Variation: Fix 2 rows of folded rose petals to conceal the pins of the Trifolds. Fix Crown flower in the centre.

Leaf & Bloom

1. **Base Preparation:**
   a) Cut a 10-inch diameter circle from a 1 1/2-inch thick thermocol sheet.
   b) Tear 25-30 two-inch wide strips from a broad banana leaf.
   c) Secure one end of each strip to the centre of the circle and the other end to the bottom using round head pins.
   d) Continue pinning the strips until the entire circle is covered.

2. **First Row:**
   a) Create a sequence of 10 Twirl foldings at a time.
   b) Fix the foldings around the edge of the circle, ensuring it is completely covered.

3. **Second and Third Rows:**
   a) Collar fold: Take a Cone and place it in the centre of a cream-colored satin ribbon, that is 1 inch wide and 3 inches long. Fold the ribbon at 45-degree angle to create a taper in the centre, then wrap it around the Cone and staple it in the centre to secure it.
   b) Fix the prepared foldings 1 inch below the first row.
   c) Fix the third row of foldings 1/2 inch below the second row, positioning them in between the previous foldings.

4. **Pin Coverage:**
   Use a green ribbon to cover the pins of the third row for a neat finish.

5. **Inversion and Fourth Row:**
   a) Invert the design, using a block of thermocol or a container for support.
   b) Fix the fourth row of Pointer foldings with three layers to the outer edge of the circle.

6. **Fifth Row:**
   Fix the same Pointer foldings in between the foldings of the fourth row.

7. **Centrepiece:**
   For the centrepiece, decorate a thermocol sphere with banana leaf Cones, Gigantea flowers, and rose petals. Secure it in the middle of the design.

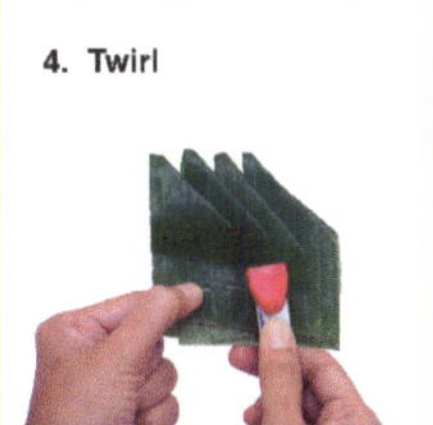

Archana Ritesh

George Vergis

Namitha Suresh

Rama B Ramamurthy

Rama B Ramamurthy

Ashwini Narsepalli

Smitha Anand

Swarnalatha Srinivas

Scorpio Charm

68

Geetha Somashekar

Kalidas Raj
Mala Kalidas

Namitha Suresh

Triveni Kasi

Gratitude to our contributors

We at Art Crumps sincerely thank everyone for lending your unique talents to enhance our banana leaf art. Your artistic contributions have added beauty and depth to our creations, and we are truly grateful for your support. Your names will forever be etched in the pages of our book.

Archana Ritesh's deft fingers bring a magical touch to everything she does. Her artistry and natural talent show the true qualities of a gifted artist.

Ashwini Srinivas is known for her captivating and unique designs. Her distinct style makes her work truly stand out.

Chaitra Supreet's radiant smile and enthusiasm makes it a joy to work with her. Her dedication and keen attention to detail are truly appreciated.

Geetha Somashekar a skilled Janur exponent has expertly brought our challenging design to life. We sincerely appreciate her invaluable participation.

George Vergis is a multifaceted artist known for his incredible versatility and speed in working with various materials. His artistic talent is truly remarkable, effortllessly transforming his ideas into stunning works of art.

Mr. Kalidas Raj and **Mrs. Mala Kalidas**, both highly skilled individuals, travelled to Indonesia, to enhance their expertise in Janur. They have graciously shared their captivating talents, adding depth and beauty to enrich our book.

Namitha Suresh excels in both Ikebana and Janur art, showcasing remarkable talent in each of them. We appreciate her passion, along with her artistic flair in both these disciplines, which has brought value to our book.

We greatly appreciate **Rama Ramamurthy's** exceptional skill and expertise in Dutch flower arrangements and thematic designs. Her boundless creativity has infused our publication with elegance and charm.

We thank **Smitha Anand** for her support in creating a few extraordinary designs for this book. Her contributions have added a special touch to the project.

Swarna Srinivas shows exceptional patience in all her works, approaching each task with calmness and focus. Her creation of strawberries with rose petals is commendable.

Triveni Kasi is highly skilled in designing beautiful backdrops using our unique motifs. Her execution reflects a keen sense of aesthetics, creating a pleasant and cohesive atmosphere.

A heartfelt thanks to…

Art Crumps sincerely values the dedication and hard work of everyone who has contributed behind the scenes, acknowledging their pivotal role in bringing our creative visions to life. We offer our heartfelt gratitude to each individual for their steadfast support and commitment.

Nithin Sagi, our photographer, excels in capturing the essence of this project. His dedication and attention to detail makes every photograph precise and beautiful.

Naveen, our second photographer, adds a fresh perspective and creativity to our project. His attention to detail gives each photograph a distinct identity.

Rohan Shivapuja efficiently and graciously resolved the challenges we encountered in operating the computer.   We are truly grateful for his expertise and willingness to help.

Chitra Sankar, our Editor, has offered valuable suggestions throughout the entire process of our book. Her insights have been essential from the start to the final completion. We are profoundly grateful to her.

Ishika Pola, the graphic designer, has played a pivotal role through her contributions in photo editing and unwavering technical support. Her dedication is deeply valued.

Jayashree Srinivas, our content writer, spent countless hours assisting in documenting the step-by-step folding techniques and notes for all the designs. Her impressive vocabulary, dedication and attention to detail are truly inspiring and commendable.   We deeply appreciate her support.